Seduction: Out of Eden

Seduction: Out of Eden

Poems by

Jaclyn Piudik and Janet R. Kirchheimer

Cover image by Johannes Rigg

ISBN: 978-1-63980-140-4

Kelsay Books
502 South 1040 East, A-119
American Fork, Utah 84003
Kelsaybooks.com

Acknowledgments

We gratefully acknowledge the print journals and online publications in which these poems, or slightly altered versions, first appeared:

"An Index of Speech" and "Staging Creation" appeared in *Bearings Online,* Collegeville Institute.

"Demure Origins" and "Fury: In Praise of Stone" appeared in *Young Ravens Literary Review.*

"Before Interpretation" and "The Hastening Blueprint" appeared in *Belmont Story Review.*

"Seduction: Out of Eden," "Creation, Redeemed," "Enditement" and "Night Monster" appeared in *Across the Margin.*

Our thanks to Ariel Grossman of the Ariel Rivka Dance company who featured "Fury: In Praise of Stone" as part of a new work entitled "No Word," which premiered in 2017 and is included in their repertory.

Contents

Opus and Inception

Pare down a reed
                    the genesis
the allegory of a bang

                that begs orchestration

                                God's embouchure

A stream fashioned by cutting

                An arrow to give birth

        The incision into chaos   a meredom of inspiration

    And we   astonished into form

Staging Creation

Bare a sheet of lightning, a barbed elusive hymn,
ethereal shimmy of sea and sky undressed; broken

blindness accompanies the husk, enfolding,
askew, as gesture descends at nightfall, arbitrary

in accomplishment. The time for assignation flutters
on ancient currents at rest. A tumult of cobalt withheld,

pending rudiment, aching for likeness in the face of
penultimate mayhem, an omen heaved from orb into ore.

Speech occupies the space of opinion and opposition;
sanguine admiration for sanctuary surges through the shade.

It is good.

With riotous heat, an imitation of order towers over
tide and benevolent hour, unbent, a hospice in darkness.

A lisp of heaven calls out and charms until morning.
Absence begins its rise in the heat of day, releases venom.

Craving elevation and delicacy of law, cogent ice lays in wait
to witness evening, morning born as one.

Structure expands, variegates into helter-skelter
imagination while apparitions ignite parables.

Vacant miracles: the mastery of raku, a token of chasms,
wet and welded, mobilize into bathwater mimesis.

Ash elides against hill, reckless, sired by substance,
meta-ocean firm and even, malleable prototype for storm clouds.

Cords splinter with aspiration, fall from leaf to leaf;
chains rust in vanity and piety, confess to failing floods.

Harboring the dusk, gentle cravings imagine broadsides,
undulate skyward, subordinate in their crescendo,

rocking samite into twilight, into beckonings,
shallow in division. A singular thirst with reticence

summons return; a woodcut relinquishes dirge,
wanders into diction: vowel-elect.

Hopeful verbiage weathers into a stretch
of elements arching for habitat. Vagrant

parallels, levitating airs, wrench to culminate
in hemistich and rarified tone; rancor is retrieved

from the depths of isolation. Consonance revives
destruction. Hydrogen suppresses isolation, pristine.

Evanescent opacity disquiets brume; primordial
emanations burgeon into lyric thronged with heat.

Sight anticipates revision. Disclosure strains
against prisons of vaulted roofs. Attributes—

cartilage bashfully arrested in buoyant springs carries
pattern mimicking sound, soul, and sunspray.

A parched architecture inquires along the shoreline. Untenanted atoms break into taut altitudes shimmering with variation.

Chocolatine atmosphere winnows into mass, ether into anatomy, spinning downward from its nest towards potential.

An Index of Speech

Presuppose time before it was a skyline

an approach-and-landing accident

an utterance of noise rarely of seraphs darkened

by clouds of astrologers' stones and emptiness

cities of frenzy groundless a line of consideration

burns itself into script onto vellum

a tower differentiated word by wing by whirr

of engine's exhale desolation into collisions

the astonishment of stars deserted blotted

on etching paper ravaged into form.

Bill of Sale

Ask now concerning days of past
                          closed on three sides   open in the front
a camera obscura   the bias of unkempt fire
           rapt in refraction from one end of heaven

                          to the other
what is worthless   what is waste
                                        Tohu
           Bohu

           the world was nothing
but water boxed in light boxed in muddle
           An instauration of voice tossing down hail

as snow becomes asphalt
                  covered by a bill of sale

A blanket of trembling steals sleep from the void: the acquisition
of wake contained in one square gasp

Before Interpretation

a vulture hovers over its young
obscurity a hiding place
where sky touches sod promising
involution newness to be plundered
breath of mouth devastated impatient
at the surface longing for the space
of distance alluvial wingspan
an extension arriving at concealment
in the havoc placed there in luxuriance
parsing possibilities azure
gradations of consequence
that crumble latent with anticipation
becoming a stammer of flight

Demure Origins

Vital memory eliminates timeshare of earth's decision;
a sheave of mist climbs as bark, petrichor, and lemonflower

usher spark into bud, a rash altruism of hearkening, a seething
contradiction. Wellsprings fracture into mercy from conversation.

The weaver dispenses herbs, constellations murmur growth,
and music preserves textual vowels; intonations explore

tousled heavens and descend to sever mystery, move fescue
to branch. Etchings of pristine vetiver, boughed, reveal up-crowded

turf ravenous for broken moisture. Anointed seedlings
trample vines where foxes break through barriers of threes.

Division lights a path among thorns and lilies.
Radical rationing of time flourishes among spheres.

Sight to be moored, beribboned in the firmament's bark,
deliberates being—between hail and hallelujah,

luster and mundanity—ulcerating the syntax of years.
A vault eclipses bdellium, elides with evidence of

consensus and suppression, reverberates in unspoiled chasm.
Retries animosity, destruction, and disclosure.

Casual in its praise, uprooted principles fragment;
designs moon-blur in stellar disagreement

to negotiate amidst cubits of infinitesimal liquid notes.
Invocations, followed by symbols, swell across interstices

awaiting ascension: an unsullied test. Humors impend,
bedecked as diglossia for attendant radiance, memorizing

greatness and minutia, gilding and stain, cosmos and cross breeze.
Carved and weighted forces enliven the foundation

of dominance, sow desolation, bound
in its giving of back-lit pleasure into practice.

A model of motion, allegorical burn, balletic. A prism
of benign refraction ordains shadow into keepsake.

The howling mire, written in borrowed skies, cradles
praxis, appellations indelible, to sow the highest alchemy.

The Hastening Blueprint

In an architecture of camouflage   to interpret matter   raw

covert   draft of resoluteness   an ability to conceive

to surface and separate ceremony from artistry   science

from solace   being from beauty   outline stretches

over an abyss   an awning embellished with compassion

a reservoir chafing the inroad to arousal by ink and aspiration

from a matrix in its own image   palaces

are built   coins struck from a single die   dust

becomes the order of time   an enigma

an aerie walled in silent interludes of beckoning and dismay

After the Void

beginning

unformed

the face of spirit

3 light
was so evening

9 waters gathered

dry land seas
herb fruit

the night
the stars

17 give 18 rule

to divide

תהו

ובהו

and evening was morning forth

waters swarm swarms fowl
fly open firmament

sea creatures   fruitful   multiply   fill waters

                         evening morning   fifth

bring the living
every kind image
            female created

       28 bless   fruitful   replenish   male   dominion

given seed   every tree shall be
      so very good

       There evening   there
            morning   six

Striking at the Wind

Measured contentment
from a gaze in contraction allows
exegesis beside the void   hurtled
from a portal of husk

seconds of eureka burn
into a reserved paradise   a distant paradox
uneven yet riddled with perfection

inevitability rhymes
with expectation and alabaster   glides

adrift   ice crackles into grateful vapor
craving blooms for surprise

leaves burst forth   marginal elixir for barrenness
themed to shade their own frightful beauty—

Heavenblind

In the glitter of storms and shadows, evening
tide gathers dispositions; clay and blood
stop their sinuous flow.

Occasion leads to the world's disarray,
a platter carved in celestial bone and rose.

One conceived of fracas, satellite of breadth invertebrate,
the refulgent terrace that ekes its heft into a sigh
of valleys, banqueted moors amidst constellations.

Reaching for sparks, they shelter in signs.
Realms created, destroyed, become gusts,
templates for squalls and thought-throes,
subtle as they are turbulent, mild as tempestuous.

Sacred veils cling to frost, restless
passion lingers from that first trice; grace
and zeal, trembling in approach, soothe a passageway.

Silence begins its reign in a haze of words.

Another borne on whispers universal ossifies
into second flesh, iris and spur, gilled in pearl,
spined in spectacle, seeking implantation.

The world is maintained.

Undertow bears thick plumage, fire conjures lumen,
wind flows to become reason.

To Forget Everything We Knew

A jumble—letters incoherent, held captive
in latticed vows—waits for query, a manifestation

of need, contextual in its remnant. Fingerprint
left on a typewriter: the backspace key.

Vehement betrothal of gloam and dawning
without witness or rival. Engram,

usher of memory shards, runs in, an offering
finned, alar; pinions ricochet unshaved of empyrean.

Vibrant with condition, tendril, gentle yet nefarious,
shakes higher, romancing welkin, shaping mist and murk

into limen. The calming airfoil hovers beyond elevation
where clouds towel creek, cascade, and brook into trope.

An espresso conclusion, antediluvian, circles,
contagious in its delivery, good in its heaving and recoiling.

To vanquish multiplicity, waves break in time;
a hierarchy—armor lost, pruned, groomed into loam.

Fulsome, mellifluous etymology of days
opines in downy thunder and wood.

The gematria of flax binds blessing; knotty
with nostalgia, cauterizes connotations, parses nurslings.

It is so. Hearth-worthy advent by waltz and bridle:
an instant commensurate with mercy.

Wildness alights, a novice craving limb, remnant
bohemian waxing toward life and reverence.

Tempests combust in permutations, knowledge—
ground thrashes in pursuit of abstractions. Protest crawls,

defiant, animate and tense with exhalation, abides
as homonym for body, reminisces over heart and mask.

Venal topos littered with turquoise and care straddles
the muck, shattering truth into saplings, breezy with deception

and infinity. A photographic consequence offers the opening
to dream, swathed among hinges, whirring past statues

quivering with pangs in verse. Mirror of relevance
nestles adamant, a bachelor to identity, maneuvering

similitude. The author begets twin and tryst to behold
the office of shadows, harmonizing hermitage with breath.

Weighted silver, a corridor of sea and shore surveyed:
conduit of hue, rebel indulgence, florid in its construct.

Bearing ascendance, a dormant iota, from beaker
to sacral blush: naked birth broods into ovum.

An earthen limp, duality acquires contour and pigment.
Angel of rain vocalizes a troubled pool with exhale.

Gnosis by Blaze

It began, a blitz in the bosom of bafflement:
braids in gentle blue-black and a gigabyte of genius
bargain for gamble. Green billows against gateways;
briars gush on a bias cut, galvanize into gold and burnt offerings.

A garden of bread and butter: grocery list for generation,

                                                 benevolent

grammar for a biosphere blessed and graceful, a glossary of

                                   becoming.

Genre broadens among gabardine grasslands, burrowing for

                                       groundswell.

Beginning is broadcast, a guarantee glistens: genus begotten.

Bioluminescence—
bride from groom, girl from boy, gift of guile; powder-blue
garters and begonias to garnish birches with ungoverned beauty.

                              [It is better.]

Grass-like benediction beguiles. Galaxies of gadabouts
garner baskets of gauze to bleed a bouquet into being.

It began with brindled geode and gases berserk with belief,

a guarantee of ground, beckoning for berth: to become God's bling.

Fury: In Praise of Stone

hewn from a quarry

a rainless summer

petrified lengths, miles

heeled in inquiry

beseeching wilderness

of converted curtains

iridescent moorings

for moisture, coupling

pebbles emerge, precious

with twilight, engraved images

of procreation spewing

[and] every yesterday

covered in light

particles arid and calm

of savage grandeur

a commencement of growth

before mercy, a realm

a roof from which to build

brittle dunes yearning

saliva with mud

foundations, stalactite beams

bare and bloody, potions

clotted with tomorrows past

still to be chiseled.

The Receiving

From wisdom, an exchange of honor breached
       the molten blue, habituated light to soma.
Quiescent and unmanifested, impossibility became

                unformed and void, darkness upon the face

boundless ether. A receptacle for prototypes.
       Odors amniotic thronged about, looked for figuration,
bondage in dimension, in bloodmark—to be swaddled in grit.

Brash mortality (its analogue unseen): a silkworm wove essence
       into body crowned with motion and terrestrial existence.
Heft of wheat and honey-scattered seed: a psalm of rain.

Astonished, requited thunder basked in illumined desire: oceans
       quivered, laid bare in release. Entwined silhouette
imploded phosphorescent; a primal point latent beyond color.

Char of white sparkled with tease and teach, breeze and breach—
       remedial flash brewing with cause. There, a world
unzipped: a furl from follicle to foliole escaping into recognition

to bandage the ripening silence. Under lock, fragments supernal
       surrounded and abided. Language expanded, a pendulum
beckoned inside sullen keyholes. Old as snow, earth reigned down

                let it unyoke the waters from the waters

imploring firmament from its shrouded crave. And through
       metallic slivers of entry, a nanosecond protracted into
moment, into luscious hour. A strangle of humidity

and eloquence ensured cohesion. Receptive germ radiated
      into fringed fire, concealed and congested. Reciprocal
enfoldment when retraction began again, again, and turned

            there was evening, and there was morning

to itself in tender recline—a wither before exposition, before
      disarray roved into whet, fulfillment. Whether weed
or appendage, aril or dermis, kernel fashioned into trace, vibrating

amidst a quorum of letters freed from limbo's apposition. They
      prevailed over equilibrium, pleated into matter: dancing
organisms, alive though unassigned, lubricated with what seeped

            male and female were created

from their very veins. Cluttered ravines, spas for sapience,
      perspired in wonder laden with offerings for barter.
Elevated and contracted, chambers splintered, animated

themselves into astral curtain: a dome of indigo'd prescience.
      Night came down, an exotic rage, surveyed its
successes, magnetized into the irreconcilable repose of afterness.

Enditement

The asking shatters, creates our likeness.
Whether to weather what is seen, heard, touched
in turmoil. Are we angels astray?
Gilded with reflection, we are sensate;
reckless in impatience, we slither
through midnight's orchard awaiting our fate
given on that sixth day. We yearn to be clad
in knowledge, warmed by logos and legacy.

Delayed in petition, a stuttering,
exquisite indigence bares divinity
into words. We face each other, split in half,
eyeing wholeness yet adrift in waking.

We fall like luminaries in pursuit
of the self, the truth that sanctifies.

A Clarity to Impulse

Gleaner of rubric—rites of obedience
ignite the breach. Fabric torn from

celestite and mystery, dripping jargon,
bares planetary wrapping for

rugged places. A salve of words
envelops worlds, wilderness

intact. There, no particle is surfeit;
each character roams to find its place.

The search for quiddity reveals a shower of grass,
heavy in umbra. Spectrum diffused brings

marks to be remembered, a boutique of engravings.
Nothing is familiar, nothing. Everything makes itself

partisan. Flickers of measure establish
remnant. Sojourn: it begins, arcs

and ebbs with momentary cry for breath.
Numbness in the before. Know this weight:

the inexorable impulse to skin lies along
dust-drifts, becomes progeny of inkling and ink.

Life is waxen, unuttered, repossessed in specks of
dirt. To clarify composition, a dizzying flush among

marshes. A vortex of testimony expands into fractal
that foretells remnants of detachment.

And with the final scuff, carapace forges
habitation, a container for mayhem, tumult borne beneath.

Night Monster

declares herself from the north corner: unfinished creation. Breaks
free as first wife. A gardener of demons and beatific gynecology.

Mother of breath, nightkeeper, hapax legomenon
dwells in a land of fruitful fields. Astonished and marked by

squalls of desire, she screeches, an owl of amazement. Banished
to the narrows, no longer fertile territory, but a world unto herself.

They call her dominatrix, an effigy to contradiction, harbinger of
dread…wildness. Messenger of alchemy, she possesses *wadis*

and kindling; brings offerings to the vineyards -~-~ dross
and crimson, wool and wine. She is faithful, pregnant

with a thousand rivers, skies once curdled and unruly,
tonguing words recognizable only on the threshold

of slumber, in the midst of daze. Drawn toward twilight,
she wanders until a luminary begins its descent along the horizon.

Parallel serf : she rises \\ to unseat anima // reflowered, rethroned
and whole. She rises † equation = she rises to puncture

the dawn : with juicy pause, blood disproven. A serpentile myth,
she drinks from a river of demons & delicate glass is sustenance.

Compassion slinks up to {ache} and liquefies into the primeval //
whirlpools she washes in each afternoon. #Lilith - - - topples

hymn, metropolis oceanic, unwithering willows with upborne tears
that defy gravity, depravity, emotion in symbol; pa~~ive no longer.

She lies prone, a golem, views the righteous that will issue
from her, hanging them

from her hair, eyes, forehead.
Sawed in half ©© during creation,

given a rib, a tail. For dignity, the tail is removed.

Cleaving

At the edge of departure, hope entices Eve.
Tree of doubt, knowledge, beckons the serpent:
Remain, reveal, sanctify, perceive.

She wavers, aroused in her will to believe.
Eden, Adam, falsehood courses through, verdant.
At the edge of departure, hope entices Eve.

With wisdom on her palate, nothing more to grieve,
she sighs; judgment precludes a lust to repent.
Remain, reveal, sanctify, perceive.

The premise of distance begins to deceive,
but truth overshadows its cunning lament.
At the edge of departure, hope entices Eve.

What is this new world that makes her want to leave?
License or an entry way into descent?
Remain, reveal, sanctify, perceive.

From idol and idyll, it is her time to cleave
inside this moment. Paradise: rent.
At the edge of departure, hope entices Eve.
Remain, reveal, sanctify, perceive.

The Night Her Sextant

Cloaked in flight, she coils around those who sleep
alone. Abandoned, she forages for amulets of rest,
incantations of shunned wasteland.

        Soldiering solitude, her fingers crusted in
        scales, lacquer, she is dreadlocked, windlocked,

    clean of servitude and diamond,
    bathing nowhere but in promise and fog.

Two halves, bought in sleep: separated, attached, severed.
Entangled in willows and alphabets of dust and gold,
she fashions a throne from alder, vipers, alliances in exile.

        A royal experience of rain undone,
        joyless yet received as sceptre, bone

    horizontal. And she lingers, malingers
    (or so they say), to escape the sear.

She stands among willows, among lions and owls.
Creature of night wings. Longing to go, exorcism
of sacred syllables brings desert retreat, children.

        The terrain of her face waved
        with worriment, not over curse

    or cursive, but abandon harbored in unjust
    ritual—a fallacious remedy for speech.

The first, wife of youth, unbridled in a compendium
of literacy, she hovers among ineffable consequence.
Anonymous sanctity brings hybrid demons and thievery.

Stripped of color, she is gray-blue shadow,
unsolicited portrait in monochrome.

What was holy is muted, now matted,
an idiom marbleized into ferocity.

Ensnared by language, she aspires to be captive to minor
epiphanies—refuses return. Bundled in wool and whimsy, aching
for messengers, monsters to lead her, she writhes among weeds.

How sweet the taste of distemper
in a bed of hemlock. A heart-stopping

warmth to defy accusation. And why not
topple illusion: a paradise cautionary or erroneous.

A barren tale of one hundred children, invisible to nomenclature.
Elemental secret of tradition, she arrives in rebellion, authored
by entanglement and ensnared in ransom.

Choosing not to bleed, she couples with hurricane
and tempest—to unravel history with thunderous

pangs, to devolve vulgarism into grievous silence. She is
the name of midnight noise, the muttering moon.

She is braided river, collar of copper rope among captive
inscriptions. Sanguine threads depict changing pathways measured
against the hour of birth, bindings alive with exterior, proclivity.

In a cache of newly coined skies, in abdication of
theology, she carves herself unseen. In a mask

of gargoyle grotesquerie, she shutters herself unnatural,
blameless for light—for creation, blameless.

The mirror ousts reflection; déjà vu thought, sound, and vision
escape their genesis in the crevasses of her rage: her trancing
celebration of things red, miracles partitioned.

Proposals like sandstone disintegrate into
reweighted heresy. Stolen waters stay latticed

in her speech. Remnant and query her meter, Lilith/she
finds her fractured home above [the] below.

Seduction: Out of Eden

A planting amidst silver-powdered vapors fades
wistful; rivers ignite, set apart, branch into a traverse

bridging line to lapse. Incendiary rufflings respire
through steam-streaked traces, biding rhythm.

Fetters of entangled vines cajole presupposition
to forsake isolation, engender name-giving clemency.

A vocabulary, vertebrate, awakens, unrelenting in its restless
infatuation. Verily stir splinters, sepia'd movements:

collaboration inures. There, in words, in apposition,
questing commences, rivals emerge, call out.

Dictum inculcates, inebriates nothingness into anima;
a gradual piercing through boundaries of sun and self.

A chronicle of sleep. Taken from essence, nexus
without volition, a leaving begins. What unfurls,

what unsettles in consciousness? New lexicon
rips open atoms and sinew to extricate disguise.

Subtle reservoirs allow thought, brushed
by knowing. Visor and vigil give way.

Beckoning to one another, ideas seek dwelling
in onomastic serenity, uninhibited integument.

Eros eyes delight, closes then opens, sews a garment.
In the cool of afternoon, hidden fruit anticipates telling, a garden

filled deep with novel yarn and yearning. Veneer falls from tissue,
from portent to dream mechanics, rousing warm exhalation.

It was good, it was evil, temptation for sight—leaves
stitched to proximity. A voice withdraws, becomes *hamsin,*

a rush of days. From above, grains feed thunder, foist thought
for procreation. And from below, a centrifuge skims blind refrain

into gradual echo hidden among trees. Where, where? Urging
for tonality, obedience, a precept that divides ardor. Naked

aspiration assigns blame, bows charisma into shame-bound
blush. One layer of skin sloughs into down, falls upward in praise.

A second melts, coagulates, girds itself with twindom, a fearless
apprentice. Arrayed in the spoils of negligence, questions abound;

answers remain desolate in their fervor. Implicated in testimony,
they conceal, they are exposed. A scrape of knife against breath,

incision into innocence. Softening mocks fictionalized encounters
between fabric and hide. Sibilance breeds narcotic beauty, allures

a pronominal sounding misfortune. A scattering of enmity will
not begin to heal; it chastens, crawls, and curses. The world takes

its shape in gravitas and labor pangs. What fertile rondure will
bequeath its molt to nourish humus and human? What organic

abundance will elucidate a footpath of pain and travail as it begins
to taint passion? A crush of rule hearkens expression and thorns.

Thistle-whisper is heard in the field, the din of a quiet motion
that slackens mindful prophecy. Comfort comes in future tense,

awakening regret for what might have been: a taste of immediacy
for tomorrow's writhing. The ground, reedy in its rupture,

brushes off return, offers its hand, forever alive in unrest, in secret
contemplation; shade copulates with light and montage breeds

its own favor. A single vertebra, a question of symmetry, pleasure
in judgement's bark. Tilled from the taking, concealment

impregnates opposition. A shattering drives them out
                    with a shudder, ecstasy turns   leaves.

Creation, Redeemed

Textured whirlwind, eastwind, leeward, sunders into garden.

Windless perfection, the rustle of inquiry leaves

only remnant of blossom and benediction; moonlit desire

ravages primeval: fetters of weeping clothed

in shelter as serpents reign rough, bemoaning Adam.

Curled vines lace while clotting into eve,

unweathered, whittled from blood-bound dusk.

With a naked flush of apotheosis, tangled oracles and gardenia

petals knit themselves mortal, coined into creation, into man.

Alone, he drowses in vertigo'd dreamstate under bough, leaf,

fruitful only in a bittersweet waltz with reflection. Clothing

himself in rarity, he discovers the warm cloak of hunger;

rivers of beguilement flow into a paradigm of wanting.

Elements pursue enclave, palpate with the mother of living things.

Eve exchanges shallows, sears adaptation, a commingling of garb

inside this hushed nursery. Shame among roots in the garden

anoints an end to youth, condemns monochrome leaves, shapes

a plait of grief. Vanity is devoured by this man of the ground.

Buried in stasis, awash in silence, prudence cannot cleanse him
of the thunders that tear through marrow, armature. Inchoate thirst
abrades, tattoos essence and extern with restless slither. Fronds
ripen his mourning for ideation, first beauty. And she, Eve,
is revivified: storehouse, progenitrix, a garden
embodied as replica. Layers of dismay become her mantle,

reflect falsehood: a shattering, primordial in its claim to vestment.
Emergent pairing, back-to-back, separated, offers this man of dust
serpentine sanctuary cleaving to mirage. Cursed into conservatory
to reveal a poultice of youth, fissure converts rapture
into a thesis that lifts and heals: the snake, the merging of Eve
with the man. A semblance crawls on its belly. Radiant, it stalks

through the syntax of union, to take refuge in temporality, leaves
pain, impermanence. Flesh stitched to flesh. Ravished threads,
disembodied, fall in rhythmic intervals. Aslink, astounded, woman
bowed under heavenness suffers no repose. Her intimate, Adam,
writhes, too. Knowing cycles, revolutions in divine longing,
they are propositions coiled together, asserting limb and greenery.

Wound-inflected prayer leaves: a hush hovers at the garden's edge;
jagged shards of anatomy scar and twist, clothed in their desire,

a labyrinth of eloquence. They mouth their names anew—

Eve, Adam.

About the Authors

Jaclyn Piudik is the author of *To Suture What Frays* (Kelsay Books 2017) and three chapbooks, *the corpus undone in the blizzard* (Espresso Chapbooks 2019), *Of Gazelles Unheard* (Beautiful Outlaw 2013) and *The Tao of Loathliness* (fooliar press 2005/8). Her poems have appeared in numerous anthologies and journals, including *New American Writing, Columbia Poetry Review, Burning House,* and *Barrow Street.* She received a New York Times Fellowship for Creative Writing and the Alice M. Sellers Award from the Academy of American Poets. Jaclyn has edited many volumes of poetry, including collections for award-winning Canadian publisher Book*hug. In addition, she edits academic monographs for the Pontifical Institute for Mediaeval Studies. She holds an M.A. in Creative Writing from the City College of New York, as well as an M.A. and collaborative Ph.D. in Medieval Studies and Jewish Studies from the University of Toronto. Jaclyn teaches creative and academic writing at the University of Toronto and has a private mentoring practice. Her website is: www.jaclynpiudik.com.

Janet R. Kirchheimer is the author of *How to Spot One of Us,* poems about the Holocaust and her family (Clal 2007). She is producing AFTER, a cinematic documentary in which poets perform and examine the role of art in responding to the Holocaust. She is a Pushcart Prize nominee with poems in numerous print and online journals and anthologies, including *Connecticut Review, Atlanta Review, Mudfish, Limestone,* and *The Poet's Quest for God.* Her chapter, "At the Water's Edge: Poetry and the Holocaust," appears in *The Psychoanalytic Textbook of Holocaust Studies* (Routledge 2019). Janet received a Certificate of Appreciation from the 261st Signal Brigade for her poetry reading for a Multi-National Forces Days of Remembrance Holocaust Memorial Service, for which she also was given a Citation from The Council of The City of New York. Most recently, she appeared at a Six-Word Memoir storytelling event at the Tenement Museum in New York City. Janet received a Drisha Institute for Jewish Education Arts Fellowship, is a writing coach, and teaches creative writing and poetry. Her website is www.janetkworks.com.

www.ingramcontent.com/pod-product-compliance
Lightning Source LLC
Chambersburg PA
CBHW071359090426
42738CB00012B/3172